W9-BHH-962

STECK-VAUGHN
PORTRAIT OF AMERICA

973
POR

Wyoming

C3

Steck-Vaughn Company

Executive Editor	Diane Sharpe
Senior Editor	Martin S. Saiewitz
Design Manager	Pamela Heaney
Photo Editor	Margie Foster

Proof Positive/Farrowlyne Associates, Inc.
Program Editorial, Revision Development, Design, and Production

Consultant: Clyde Douglass, Assistant Director, Wyoming Tourism

Published by Raintree Steck-Vaughn Publishers, an imprint of Steck-Vaughn Company.

A Turner Educational Services, Inc. book. Based on the Portrait of America television series by R. E. (Ted) Turner.

Cover Photo: Mountain landscape by © Michael Reagan.

Library of Congress Cataloging-in-Publication Data

Thompson, Kathleen.
    Wyoming / Kathleen Thompson.
      p. cm. — (Portrait of America)
    "Based on the Portrait of America television series" — T.p. verso.
    "A Turner book."
    Includes index.
    ISBN 0-8114-7397-X (library binding). — ISBN 0-8114-7478-X (softcover)
    1. Wyoming—Juvenile literature. [1. Wyoming.] I. Title. II. Series:
Thompson, Kathleen. Portrait of America.
F761.3.T48 1996
978.7—dc20

95-25729
CIP
AC

Printed and Bound in the United States of America

4 5 6 7 8 9 10 WZ 03 02 01 00

Acknowledgments
The publishers wish to thank the following for permission to reproduce photographs:
Pp. 7, 8 Wyoming Division of Tourism; pp. 10, 11 American Heritage Center, University of Wyoming; p. 12 Wyoming Division of Tourism; p. 14 (both) American Heritage Center, University of Wyoming; pp. 15, 16, Wyoming State Archives, Department of Museums and History; p. 17 (top) Wyoming State Archives, Department of Museums and History, (bottom) American Heritage Center, University of Wyoming; p. 19 © Michael Reagan; pp. 20, 21, 22, 23 Wyoming Wool Growers Association; p. 24 © Leda Price; p. 26 © Dan Abernathy/Profiles West; pp. 28, 29 © Michael Reagan; p. 30 Holly Sugar Corporation; p. 31 © Hal Sommer; p. 33 © Marilyn Boone; p. 34 © Larry Ulrich/Tony Stone Images; p. 36 (top) Buffalo Bill Historical Center, (bottom) National Park Service; p. 37 (both) Pete Saloutos/Wyoming Division of Tourism; p. 38 © Robert Bakker/Snake River Institute; p. 39 © National Audubon Society; p. 40 © Jim Allen/Allen's Diamond Four Ranch; p. 41 © National Audubon Society; p. 42 © Wiley Wales/Profiles West; p. 44 National Park Service; p. 46 One Mile Up; p. 47 (left) One Mile Up, (center) National Wildflower Research Center, (right) © A. Carey/Vireo.

STECK-VAUGHN
PORTRAIT OF AMERICA

Wyoming

Kathleen Thompson

A Turner Book

RSVP

RAINTREE
STECK-VAUGHN
PUBLISHERS

The Steck-Vaughn Company

Austin, Texas

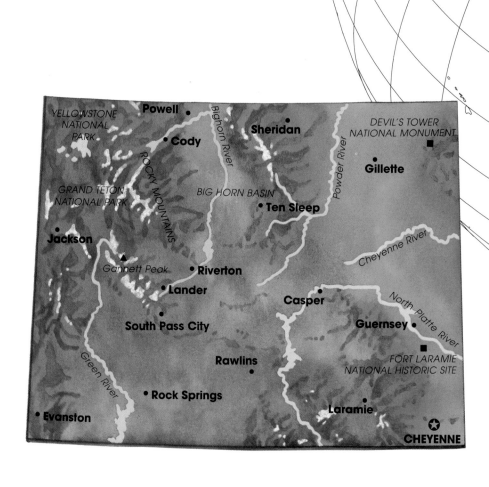

Wyoming

Powell

Cody

YELLOWSTONE
NATIONAL
PARK

ROCKY MOUNTAINS

Bighorn River

Sheridan

Powder River

DEVIL'S TOWER
NATIONAL MONUMENT

Gillette

GRAND TETON
NATIONAL PARK

BIG HORN BASIN

Ten Sleep

Jackson

Cheyenne River

Gannett Peak

Riverton

Lander

Casper

North Platte River

South Pass City

Guernsey

Green River

Rawlins

FORT LARAMIE
NATIONAL HISTORIC SITE

Rock Springs

Laramie

Evanston

CHEYENNE

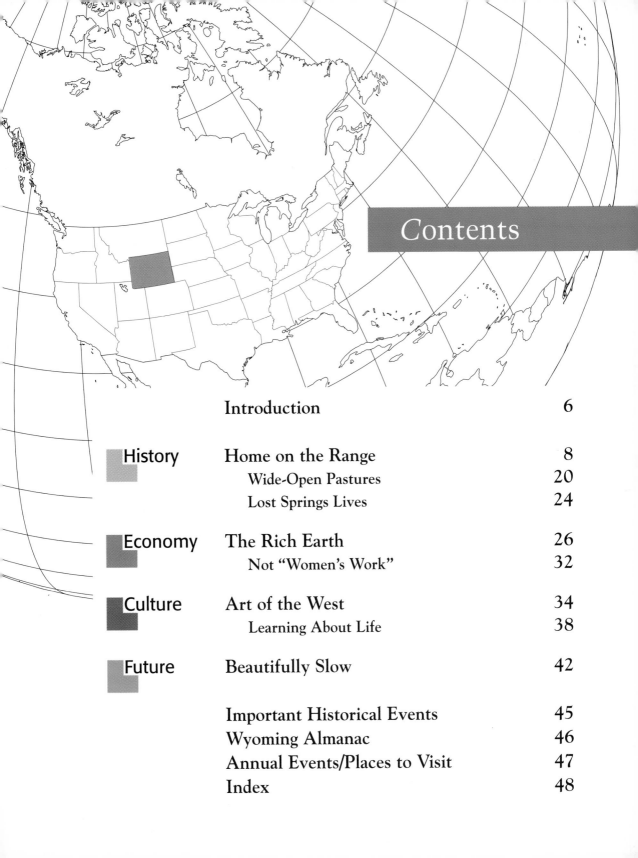

Contents

Introduction

Wyoming has a history as big and wild as its landscape. Its vast plains were once home to great Native American groups, such as the Sioux and the Arapaho. Its large wide-open spaces were an invitation to pioneers to take hold of its boundless beauty and settle down. Trails that were opened in Wyoming brought people from distant places. In 1869 Wyoming showed its commitment to equal rights by becoming the first state to give women the opportunity to vote. Wyoming has kept the best of its past in the years since. Its small population works hard to preserve equal rights as well as the natural beauty of the land. What's important to the people of Wyoming is basic—open land and freedom.

Mount Moran, as viewed from the Snake River, is a perfect example of the rugged beauty of Wyoming.

Wyoming

Home on the Range

By 1700 the place we now call Wyoming was home to Sioux, Arapaho, Crow, Blackfeet, Bannock, Cheyenne, Shoshone, and Ute. In the Bighorn Mountains, these Native Americans trapped beaver. On the Great Plains, they hunted buffalo. They killed these animals not only for their meat but also for their skins. In fact, they used the entire animal. The Native Americans preserved meat by hanging it to dry in the sun. They used the skins to make teepees, blankets, and robes. Buffalo bones were carved into knives; hooves and horns were boiled into glue. They even used the buffalo's tendons for bowstrings.

In 1806 Meriwether Lewis and William Clark passed close to present-day Wyoming on their way to the Pacific Ocean. In 1807 a member of the Lewis and Clark expedition named John Colter left the group. On his way back across the continent, Colter set out into the Wyoming wilderness to do some trapping. He was captured by Native Americans but managed to escape. He crossed the Continental Divide in 1807 and finally found

The early pioneers who settled in present-day Wyoming had to endure loneliness in an underpopulated land. Very often the nearest neighbor would live as much as ten miles away.

Lewis and Clark are shown here with Sacagawea, the Shoshone woman who guided them to the Pacific Ocean. John Colter is standing in the far left of the picture.

his way to the area now designated as Yellowstone National Park. It's impossible to imagine what John Colter felt as he walked alone through the fossil forests, stood before the black glass mountain, and watched the hot springs steam and the geysers erupt. He saw one of the most astonishing natural wonderlands in the world. He was seeing sights that none of the settlers had ever seen before. When he got back to the East Coast, people did not believe such fantastic things could occur on Earth.

A few years later, the Wilson Hunt Price expedition passed through present-day Wyoming on its way to the mouth of the Columbia River. Because they were hired by John Jacob Astor of the American Fur Company, these fifty or sixty fur traders were called the Astorians. In 1812 some of that party, led by Robert Stuart, returned through the area and discovered the South Pass.

Soon fur traders and trappers began to find their way to this beautiful wilderness of the North. William Ashley of the Rocky Mountain Fur Company advertised for men to come to the Wyoming country. He reated the fur traders' rendezvous. The rendezvous was a place where the company brought supplies to trade for furs. It was also the great social event of the frontier. Once a year in the spring, Native Americans, trappers, and traders met to drink, dance, and tell stories. The rendezvous usually lasted for a week or two before everyone went back to their usual business.

In 1824 the Rocky Mountain Fur Company men started using the South Pass as a way through the mountains. The South Pass is a valley along the Oregon Trail. It was a way to get through the Rocky Mountains without having to climb them. For the next half century, increasing numbers of pioneers took one of three wagon trails through the South Pass.

Four main wagon trails snaked through Wyoming—the Oregon Trail, the Mormon Trail, the California Trail, and the Overland Trail. The Oregon Trail began in Independence, Missouri. The Mormon and California trails followed the Oregon Trail west and took the South Pass through the mountains. The South Pass lay just a little southwest of the center of Wyoming. From there the Mormon Trail veered southwestward to reach the Mormon colony in the region of the Great Salt Lake in present-day Utah. The California Trail eventually ended at Sutter's Mill in present-day Sacramento. The Oregon Trail traveled northwest to Fort Vancouver in Oregon Territory. The Overland Trail took a more southerly route across Wyoming and then joined other trails at Fort Bridger.

In 1834 Robert Campbell and William Sublette built Fort William near the point where the Platte and

This is an early color photograph of geysers at Yellowstone National Park. Yellowstone has been a popular tourist attraction for more than a century.

Laramie rivers meet. They sold it to the American Fur Company, and it became the first permanent non-Native American settlement in Wyoming. Later the United States government bought the fort, renamed it Fort Laramie, and turned it into a military post.

The traders and the trappers got along well with the Native Americans. The fur traders had no interest in taking away the Native Americans' land. Even the early pioneers bound for California and Oregon presented no threat. The Native Americans even assisted the first small wagon trains and traded with them. But soon larger wagon trains and permanent settlers came into Wyoming. The growing population caused problems for the Native Americans because the settlers were no longer guests—they were intruders.

In 1835 a pair of Methodist missionary brothers, Jason and Daniel Lee, opened what was then called the Oregon Country to farming. They traveled across

Fort Laramie was the site of treaty councils between Native Americans and the United States government. Today, it is a National Historic Site.

Wyoming by means of the Oregon Trail. The first few travelers were soon followed by others from farther east who intended to settle in and begin farming.

John C. Frémont led a government expedition into the area in 1842 and reported that the West was not a barren wilderness but a land of opportunity. Copies of his report were published and circulated, and in 1843 Marcus Whitman led a great wagon train of settlers over the Oregon Trail. The wagon train consisted of 120 wagons, more than a thousand people, and over five thousand head of cattle. The great westward migration had begun!

In 1847 Brigham Young led a large group of Mormons along the Mormon Trail through Wyoming to present-day Utah. When gold was discovered in California in 1849, thousands of "Forty-Niners" followed the California Trail hoping to find their fortunes in the gold mines.

In the years that followed, the Oregon Trail was the path of stage and mail coaches, the pony express, and the telegraph. In a sense, it was the Oregon Trail that opened up the West. The Oregon Trail offered plentiful water, good grazing land, and a relatively easy passage through the rugged mountains.

Not everyone was happy about this new path to the frontier, however. The people whose land it crossed—the Native Americans—were very angry. They attacked wagons and stagecoaches that traveled along the Oregon Trail. Finally, the stage line was moved south to the Overland Trail, and soldiers were sent out to protect the settlers.

A contemporary painting shows Native Americans camped outside a United States Army outpost.

Chief Red Cloud led the Sioux in battles against the settlers who invaded their lands in the 1860s.

A treaty signed in 1851 was supposed to make peace between settlers and Native Americans. But the settlers often did not keep their agreements. Fighting broke out again and again.

When gold was discovered in Montana, the government sent troops to protect the Bozeman Trail. The trail was a 600-mile path to the mines between Fort Laramie, Wyoming, and Virginia City, Montana. The troops set up military posts, Fort Phil Kearny and two others, right in the middle of the Sioux hunting ground. The Sioux, led by Red Cloud, again fought to protect their lands. In December 1866, Red Cloud lured a cavalry regiment led by Captain William J. Fetterman deep into the wilderness near the Wyoming-Montana border. Red Cloud then led his people in an ambush of the regiment, killing all 82 soldiers. The Fetterman ambush and other similar attacks caused a public debate across the country about controlling the Native Americans.

In 1867 a Peace Commission was set up. The commission's solution was to close the Bozeman Trail and isolate the Native Americans on small reservations. That same year the Shoshone, led by Chief

Washakie, agreed to move to the Wind River Reservation.

But the Native Americans who had been forced onto reservations refused to stay there. Settlers invaded the Black Hills, a sacred land for many Native American nations. Fighting began again. In 1876, Dull Knife, Crazy Horse, Two Moons, and Sitting Bull made one last try to keep their land. They won a major battle at the Little Bighorn River, just across the border in Montana. Their victory was over Lieutenant Colonel George Custer's troops. Reaction across the country to "Custer's Last Stand" was outrage. A few months later, the Sioux were overcome and defeated. Native American hopes for the future in Wyoming and throughout the West were crushed.

In the meantime, the population of Wyoming was growing. Gold was discovered at South Pass, and that brought in several thousand miners. Another transportation route was created that would prove as important as the Oregon Trail—a railroad across the country. From 1867 to 1868, workers cleared a path and laid down tracks for the Union Pacific Railroad to come through southern Wyoming.

In April 1868 the government organized the area as the Wyoming Territory. On December 10, 1869, Wyoming women became the first women in this country—and in most of the world—to gain the right to vote. Women had struggled across the country by covered wagon. They had worked side by side with their husbands on farms and ranches. They had risked death by starvation, exposure, and disease. To the men

Captain William J. Fetterman and his troops were killed by the Sioux in 1866. The public protest against the massacre and other Native American attacks caused Congress to create a Peace Commission in 1867 to seek an end to the Sioux War.

15

Wyoming's first railroad line, the Union Pacific, was completed in 1868. This photo of the Cheyenne train depot was taken twenty years later.

in the territorial legislature, it made sense that women should have the right to vote, too. Women in the rest of the country waited another fifty years to be able to vote. In 1889 a constitutional convention was assembled at Cheyenne. Wyoming became the forty-fourth state in the Union one year later.

At first, there weren't many farmers in Wyoming. There were mostly ranchers. The rolling plains were perfect for cattle. There was plenty of grass for them to eat, and the grass lasted through the winter. By 1880 bosses of cattle drives that originated in Texas were herding their cattle to graze on the Wyoming range. The cattle were then loaded onto boxcars and shipped east on the Union Pacific Railroad.

The high profits brought by the cattle caused some problems. Cattle overcrowded the range. Also, rustlers began raiding the herds. Then, in the winter of 1887, temperatures dropped so low that about 75% of the cattle died from lack of water and food as well as exposure to bitter weather. Cattle died by the tens of thousands. Many ranches closed.

By the 1890s, farmers, or homesteaders, began moving into Wyoming. They claimed pieces of land on which to build farms and built fences around their fields and waterholes. The day of the open cattle range was over.

The ranchers did not happily accept this fact. They fought against the homesteaders. In 1892 ranchers and farmers battled each other in the Johnson County War. The ranchers claimed that the homesteaders were stealing and keeping the ranchers' cattle for their own use. As a result, the ranchers organized a private army of about fifty-five men. They killed two homesteaders. The homesteaders responded by setting up an armed force of their own. The United States Army was needed to break up the fight. Afterward fences went up around the ranches, too.

From about 1900 to 1910, the population of Wyoming grew quickly. Many ranchers began raising sheep instead of cattle. People came to mine coal, build railroads, and farm land. Oil deposits had been discovered in the state. The state's first successful oil well was drilled in 1883, near Lander in west-central Wyoming.

Wyoming was the first state to grant women the right to vote. This drawing shows a scene at a Cheyenne polling place in 1888.

A private army of gunmen was hired by cattle ranchers to force homesteaders off the range, leading to the Johnson County War.

Then, in 1912 a major strike north of Casper started Wyoming's first oil boom.

In the 1930s the country's economy collapsed in what became known as the Great Depression. More than 13 million people across the country were unemployed. Banks and other financial institutions closed and then slowly reopened. Wyoming's oil production helped the state get through the financial crunch. Federal irrigation and hydroelectric projects also put many people to work. When the United States became involved in World War II in 1941, the state's economy was given a much-needed boost. Suddenly demand skyrocketed for meat, lumber, coal, and oil. Wyoming had all these goods in abundance.

After World War II Wyoming began mining two increasingly important minerals—uranium and trona. Uranium is needed to build atomic bombs and nuclear power plants. Trona contains sodium carbonate, which is used to produce glass, soap, and paper. Until about 1960 both the mineral mining and oil-refining operations grew gradually but steadily. During the 1960s the state's population remained steady.

Wyoming's population increased by 41 percent in the 1970s. A worldwide energy crisis was partially responsible for this rapid growth rate. United States reserves of coal and petroleum suddenly became very important, and more people were needed to work in the industry. The sudden rush of people created housing shortages and overcrowding in the mining communities. All of a sudden, after mostly slow, steady growth for nearly a century, Wyoming was experiencing some of

A weathered barn stands against a clear Wyoming sky. In many places in Wyoming, the past seems very close to the present.

the problems associated with the faster-growing, more-industrialized states.

New concerns for the environment took major priority in the 1980s. The burning of fossil fuels—oil and coal—was decreased substantially. Nuclear power development was nearly at a standstill. By the time the energy crisis ended, Wyoming actually had decreased in population.

In 1980 Wyoming had fewer people than any state except Alaska. By 1990 Alaska had more people. Wyoming not only had the fewest people of any state but also fewer people per square mile than any state except Alaska. Residents, however, were beginning to think that wasn't such a bad thing. Other states that had grown larger and faster were starting to have problems. Their water and air were polluted. Their forests were cut down. Their hills and mountains were dotted with houses. They had huge, overcrowded, crime-ridden cities.

But Wyoming is different. Wyoming has remained relatively clean and wild. Much of the state still offers the beautiful landscapes that were familiar to the Native Americans and earliest settlers two centuries ago.

Wide-Open Pastures

When you drive through the wide-open pastures of Wyoming, you'll probably see sheep and cattle grazing side by side. But it wasn't always that way. Not so long ago, cattle ranchers and sheep ranchers did not get along. More than once, their dislike erupted into bloody violence.

Sheep had been grazing on Wyoming land almost from the time the first pioneers came from the East. Since they are small animals, sheep do not eat as much grass as cattle. Sheep are hardy and well-suited to the high plains that cover much of Wyoming. They also are a source of wool and meat. Heavy wool garments from Wyoming sheep helped the settlers survive the harsh mountain winters.

At first there was enough land for both sheep and cattle. Sheep could graze in the higher elevations where the grass was nutritious enough for them. Cattle ranged in the lower prairie lands. But as the population of the state grew and ranches got larger, this system didn't always work. Some cattle ranchers said their herds were dying of thirst because cattle wouldn't

People have been raising sheep for their wool for thousands of years.

On a modern ranch, one sheep can produce ten pounds of wool per year.

drink from the same water supply where sheep had drunk. They said that cattle couldn't graze land where sheep flocks had grazed. Some so-called experts even said that sheep and cattle just naturally hated each other!

Today we know that all these stories are false. Even a century ago, many people knew they weren't true. In fact some cattle ranchers actually kept small flocks of sheep for extra income. But sometimes truth has a hard time winning out over rumors.

Several genuine problems did exist, however. Sheep eat the grass down closer to the ground than cattle do. In addition, sheep's sharp hooves destroy what little they don't eat. After sheep have grazed, it takes a long time for the grass to grow back. Grass that supports cattle, however, is never eaten completely away.

In addition, most of the cattle ranchers led stable, stationary lives in permanent houses. They were a part of their communities. In contrast, many of the sheepherders had no fixed residence at all. They lived in wagons that were like horse-drawn house trailers. They followed their flocks across the open range and moved from place to place whenever the sheep did.

These sheepherders would show up, allow their sheep to eat all the grass, and then move on. It's easy to see why the cattle ranchers didn't like that.

Finally, most of the cattle ranchers and cowboys were of British descent. Their ancestors had come to America from England, Scotland, or Ireland. But many of the sheepherders came from other places. They were Mexican, Portuguese, French, and even Chinese. Some were Basques. The Basque people come from a small area in the mountains between France and Spain.

The language they speak is completely different from any other language in the world. In their mountainous homeland, many Basques are sheepherders. So it was only natural that they'd become sheepherders and follow their traditional way of life in the mountains of the American West.

One Basque who is a sheepherder in Wyoming today says, "The first Basque here in Johnson County was my great-uncle. He came here in 1904. Then, when he came back home, he told everyone, 'That is a nice country over there. Why don't you come over?' In those days there were no fences, no highways, just wide-open country."

Unfortunately, some people dislike anyone who looks different or speaks a different language. So the fact that many of the sheepherders did not speak English led to violence.

The violence began in the early 1870s. Ranchers rode into sheepherders' camps and scattered their flocks. It soon grew worse. Roving bands of "nightriders" began killing the sheep and the dogs that guarded them. They burned the sheepherders' wagons. Usually they didn't harm the sheepherders.

But gradually that changed. Nightriders started dragging sheepherders from their wagons and beating them. The sheepherders began carrying guns and fighting back. At times the conflict resembled a small war.

The final bloody incident occurred on April 2, 1909. It was known as the "Ten Sleep Raid." Five sheepherders and about six thousand sheep were camped near the town of Ten Sleep in north-central Wyoming. Cattlemen attacked in the night without warning, shooting into the wagons. Three of the sheepherders were killed. One of the attackers, feeling guilty, told investigators who had committed the raid. In the end, five cattle ranchers were convicted of the crime. Today, ranchers and sheepherders live side by side as friends and neighbors. They realize that their shared need to keep their land productive is far more important than any differences they once had.

Most sheep in Wyoming are raised on large ranges in the mountainous areas in the western region of the state.

23

Lost Springs Lives

When you think of a small town, how many people do you picture living there? A thousand? One hundred? A town of one hundred people would be smaller than nearly any town in the United States.

But in east-central Wyoming, on U.S. Highway 18-20, the town of Lost Springs has a total of three permanent residents! And yes, it's a real town. It was incorporated in 1911.

Leda Price has been mayor of Lost Springs for more than ten years. She was born in Wisconsin but came to Wyoming after high school. The town's two other permanent residents are Robert and Clair Stringham, both of whom have lived there for more than 25 years. They run the post office and

Leda Price is mayor of a town of three people. She also owns the town's tavern, rents trailers to vacationers . . . and occasionally milks a cow.

own Lost Springs' only store—an antique shop. Besides serving as mayor, Leda Price owns and operates the town's tavern in a building that once was a bank. She lives upstairs. Some of the tavern's fixtures were owned by the family of Doc Holliday, the famous gunman who took part in the "Gunfight at the O.K. Corral." Leda prepares food for parties, rents trailers to hunters and construction workers, and sells fishing and hunting licenses.

"People wonder how a town the size of Lost Springs can survive," she says. "Well, we're the 'home town' for all the ranches in the area." Most of the ranches have been owned by the same families for several generations. Many of the owners are sixty and seventy years old and still actively work their ranches. Amazingly, most of their children and grandchildren haven't moved away and are staying on their family land. "This is a very close-knit group," says Leda Price.

Lost Springs has no police force and no taxes. The Converse County sheriff's department handles any crime, and the state and the county provide whatever municipal funds are needed. The town also has no grocery store. Leda Price shops either in Lusk, a town of fifteen hundred people 25 miles to the east, or Douglas, a town of five thousand people 29 miles to the west.

Lost Springs' biggest event is an antique auction that has been held in June for the past 14 years. Each year the auction draws more than five hundred people, many of whom drive in from out of state.

Leda Price is certain that, small as it is, Lost Springs will still be alive and well twenty years from now. She says there is a whole new generation of newborn babies on the ranches, and that "people are always inquiring about living in Lost Springs." Perhaps they like the idea of living in what might be the smallest incorporated town in the country. Or possibly they just agree with Leda Price, who says, "I don't think you could live in a better neighborhood anywhere."

The Rich Earth

Wyoming is a young state, just about a century old. Two hundred years ago, the people living in Wyoming found that everything they needed was provided by the earth. Today the people of Wyoming still look to the land for their living. The state's most important resources aren't huge factories, financial centers, or retail shopping malls. They are the gifts of the land: minerals, grazing land, scenery, wildlife, and water.

In the middle of the last century, major gold and coal mines were active in Wyoming. Today coal ranks third in value behind the state's deposits of petroleum and natural gas. Much of the coal is buried too far underground to be worth mining at current coal prices. These days the mineral that fuels the state's economy is oil. The state has thousands of oil wells. These oil wells are spread throughout 21 of the state's 23 counties.

When you add Wyoming's other minerals, mining accounts for over $3.5 million per year, almost 30% of the state's gross product. That's one of the highest

These cowboys are rounding up cattle. Part of their job is to brand the newborn calves and select the cows to be sold for beef.

About half of Wyoming's land is used for grazing by livestock such as sheep and cattle.

percentages of any state, and it makes mining the state's leading single source of income. Other minerals include bentonite, trona, gemstones, and gypsum.

Service industries make up more than half of Wyoming's economy. Service industries are those in which workers serve other people instead of making a product. Service industries include transportation, communication, utility companies, financial and real estate businesses, government services, and wholesale and retail selling. Personal services such as those provided by doctors, lawyers, hotels and resorts, and repair shops are counted among the state's service industries, too. State and federal governments are

Sheep are gathered for springtime shearing in Buffalo. Wyoming is one of the nation's leading wool-producing states.

Wyoming's largest providers of service industry jobs. One such employment resource is the air force base near Cheyenne. The state's huge expanse of publicly owned lands also employs thousands of rangers, conservationists, and tour guides.

Agriculture accounts for a fairly small percentage of the state's income, but it is a very important part of the economy. When cowboys herded cattle up from Texas, they set the pattern for the state's agriculture. Most of the agriculture in Wyoming is ranching. Grazing land takes up about half of the land in the state. Much of this is federal land leased to ranchers. Although the beef industry is still the most important part of the state's agriculture, Wyoming is also one of the nation's largest sheep and wool producers.

Most of the crops in Wyoming are grown on irrigated land. They include hay, sugar beets, wheat, corn, beans, potatoes, and barley. Just about all of the hay is grown to feed Wyoming's cattle when bad weather prevents them from grazing.

Sugar beets, one of the state's major crops, are grown on this Wyoming farm.

Compared to most of the states, Wyoming doesn't have much manufacturing. You won't find rows of factories. There are factories, of course, but they are less important to the economy than in any other state except Alaska. Most of Wyoming's factories process the resources of the land. There are petroleum refineries, chemical factories, food-processing plants, and sawmills.

There is one other way that Wyoming's land is important to the state's economy. People come to look at it—to sail, camp, hike, and ride in it and simply to appreciate the peaceful solitude. Very early in the state's history, Wyoming's leaders realized that people would come to see the scenery. The leaders also realized that if they didn't take steps to preserve that beauty, it could be lost forever. Yellowstone was the world's first national park. It was created in 1872, even before

Wyoming became a state. This park was followed by the country's first national forest. The Shoshone National Forest was dedicated in 1891. The first national monument, Devil's Tower, was dedicated in 1906. Today the millions of tourists who come to gaze at the Old Faithful geyser in Yellowstone or to camp in the mountains bring in more than a billion dollars every year.

In far more ways than the Native Americans or first pioneers ever dreamed, Wyoming's rich land is still taking good care of its people. Wyoming's natural resources are also its main economic product. This will help ensure that the state will preserve not only its beauty but also its resourcefulness.

Yellowstone's famed geysers attract millions of tourists to this national park each year.

Not "Women's Work"

There are lots of jokes about women truck drivers. But for many years at the Cordero Mining Company in Gillette, Wyoming, no one told any to Marilyn Boone. That's because she drove a truck so huge it would scare most people.

"The size of it is almost unbelievable" said Marilyn. "It's so big, it feels like you're driving an apartment house."

Most trucks that size are driven by men. But Wyoming has a long history of being in the forefront of women's rights. It allowed women the right to vote in 1869. That was more than fifty years before women got that right nationwide.

With that kind of history, it isn't too surprising to see a woman driving the huge trucks that haul coal out of the mine pits. When Marilyn's company looked for a driver, they didn't worry about whether it would be a man or a woman. They just wanted someone who could do the job.

"When my husband was alive, he used to get a big kick out of the fact that I drove that truck," Marilyn recalled. "We would be out in public somewhere and I would be all dolled up in my velvet jacket and skirt and he'd say, 'Do you know what this lady does for a living?' And then he would pull out a picture of me beside my truck."

But Marilyn didn't go after the job as a truck driver so she could surprise people. She just wanted better pay than she was getting as a secretary. So she applied for the job and got it.

Marilyn found out she enjoyed driving a truck, and she stayed with the job for years. But she still remembers what people said to her when she started out.

"When I first decided to come to the pit from the secretarial pool, a lot of the administrative people told me, 'But you'll get so dirty.' Of all the things they could have objected to, I thought that was the silliest. So my standard reply was, 'But with the good salary that I'll be making driving that big truck, I can afford to buy a lot of soap.'"

Marilyn Boone showed all the people with objections and jokes about women drivers that she could do the job. And all across Wyoming today, women are doing jobs that people used to think of as "men's work," and showing that they can do just fine.

Standing next to the truck she drove, Marilyn Boone barely comes up to the middle of one wheel. This is one of the largest trucks in the world.

Art of the West

There have been many stories told about the pioneers who crossed the Rockies. There are legends of gold miners and ranchers who made their mark in the Old West. Perhaps in an effort to keep the truth separate from the fiction, Wyoming has more than fifty museums scattered throughout the state.

Most of Wyoming's museums relate to the state's history and its heritage as part of the Old West. One example is the Whitney Gallery of Western Art at the Buffalo Bill Historical Center in Cody. Buffalo Bill's real name was William F. Cody. The Whitney Gallery has a fine collection of work by western artists such as Frederic Remington, Charles Russell, and Albert Bierstadt. These artists are known around the world for their realistic and often stirring images of life in the Old West. There are no photographs before about 1840. So we must rely on the imaginations and the abilities of artists to show us what life must have been like on the frontier.

Lower Falls, in Yellowstone National Park's Grand Canyon, is 308 feet high.

above. "Where Great Herds Come to Drink" is the name of this oil painting by famed Western artist Charles M. Russell. It hangs in the Whitney Gallery of Western Art in Cody.

below. Wyoming is famous for giving visitors a chance to see wildlife in its natural setting. These bears are in Yellowstone National Park.

The Whitney Gallery is not the only museum at the Buffalo Bill Center. The site actually houses three other museums. All of them bring to life the adventure—and the hardship—of the Old West. The Buffalo Bill Museum displays William F. Cody's guns, saddles, clothing, and personal items. It also features posters and photographs from his famous Wild West Show. The Plains Indian Museum portrays the Native Americans' way of life. Exhibits show relics from the time when Sioux, Cheyenne, Shoshone, Crow, Arapaho, and Blackfeet lived in Wyoming. The Cody Firearms Museum exhibits many of the guns that were used in the Old West.

The National Museum of Wildlife Art in Jackson contains the world's largest collection of paintings and sculptures of animals native to the western United States. From the majestic buffalo and elk to fish and birds, if it walked, swam, flew, or crawled in the West, it's probably in this museum.

Some of Wyoming's most fascinating museums aren't within four walls. South of Guernsey is the Oregon Trail Ruts State Historic Site Landmark. For many years, the early westbound wagons were forced by rock outcroppings to travel exactly the same path. Today, 150 years later, you can still see the ruts their wheels made in the prairie sandstone! Another such landmark can be seen at Independence Rock, fifty miles southwest of Casper. More than five thousand travelers along the Oregon Trail inscribed their names at this place. They left a permanent record of their epic journey west.

These children are about to perform a traditional Shoshone dance.

Wyoming culture does not live only in the past, however. The Wyoming Arts Council and the Wyoming Artists Association see to that. The Wyoming Artists Association, for example, sponsors art shows in small towns around the state, and the Arts Council sponsors various arts activities. In the Jackson Hole area alone there are more than 35 art galleries. They feature paintings, sculpture, pottery, and photographs by modern-day Wyoming artists.

In Wyoming the finest sculpture and the most beautiful colors are created by nature. Most artists' creations pale in comparison to the sensational beauty of the Grand Tetons and Yellowstone National Park. In a way, Wyoming is a museum of nature's art.

Peaceful reflections give quiet beauty to this view of the Grand Tetons and the Snake River.

Learning About Life

There are schools in Wyoming that teach children and adults a lot more than the ABCs. These schools teach students hands-on lessons about nature and the great outdoors. What makes these schools especially unique is that their classrooms are out in nature.

The Snake River Institute in Jackson Hole, Wyoming, has a variety of summer courses for people ages 6 through 13. The institute is a center for learning, and its classes take place all over the Rocky Mountain region. These courses offer challenging new ways to be creative while exploring nature. Participants choose from a wide variety of programs and activities. For example, some courses focus on Native American culture and crafts, tracks and trails, natural clues to seasonal changes, and outdoor cooking. Students learn from artists, storytellers, ranchers, gardeners, and other experts.

These people are unearthing the bones of a dinosaur! They are participating in a Snake River Institute program called "Big Bones of Central Wyoming."

The Audubon Ecology Workshop features lectures in mountain ecology. The setting is in a mountain valley, 7,500 feet high in the Wind River Mountains.

There are also expeditions children can go on with their parents. One of these expeditions is called Fossil Excavation for Families. On this trip, families dig to look for fossil fish, plants, and other remains. Not a lot of fish in the mountains of Wyoming, you say? Actually, about sixty million years ago, Wyoming was under a vast tropical lake! An expert is on hand to help you identify and date any fossils found.

Another family adventure is panning for gold. The institute takes people on a three-and-a-half day trip to the gold mines of South Pass, Atlantic Gulch, Miners' Delight, and Lewiston. The trip includes lessons in gold panning. If while panning you're lucky enough to find any gold, it's yours to take home.

Allen's Diamond Four Ranch, outside of Lander, is another back-country summer "classroom" for boys and girls. It is geared to students ages 9 to 15. The main event at the Diamond Four Ranch is the Youth Pack Trip, which begins high in the spectacular Wind River Range. On the trip children learn tent pitching, map reading, and other wilderness skills.

39

Students ride horses along part of the historic Oregon Trail, the route many pioneers took in their journey to the West. The Oregon Trail stretched for two thousand miles, beginning in Independence, Missouri, and ending in Vancouver, Washington. Luckily, participants don't have to go quite that far! But they *do* camp at some pretty interesting spots along the way.

One campsite is a deserted pony express station. The pony express was a short-lived experiment in mail delivery that took place in 1860 and 1861.

Sacks of mail were taken across the United States on horseback. There were 190 stations along the route. A rider arrived at a station and handed the mail over to another rider. That person galloped off to the next station on a fresh horse. Campers today pitch their tents right next to one of these stations and imagine what it was like over one hundred years ago.

The Youth Pack Trip also takes some time off from trail riding and camping to do a little fishing and swimming in the Sweetwater River.

At the Great Plains Wildlife Institute, tourists can help naturalists and biologists with field research projects and animal population surveys.

ese people are collecting
ects at the Audubon Ecology
rkshop. Participants spend
t of their time studying
ds, mammals, insects, and
vers.

e trip takes them through some of
s country's most dazzling scenery.
rrow passes, snowcapped moun-
ns, and icy, clear streams are just a
v of the sights along the way.

There are other outdoor schools,
titutes, and workshops in Wyoming.
any that are geared toward adults
e more like college courses. One
ch school is the week-long Audubon
ology Workshop in the Rockies.
agine a valley located 7,500 feet
jh in the Wind River Mountains.
rrounding your cabin are snowy
aks rising 13,000 feet into the air. At
jht it seems that you can see every
r in the clear sky. By day students

learn about protecting birds, plants,
and animals. Students also look for
petroglyphs. These are pictures or
symbols that Native Americans carved
into walls long ago. Native Americans
in Wyoming did not write their spoken
language, and they often described
what they saw through these petroglyphs. The workshop also allows time
for hiking, fishing, and canoeing.

Wyoming is not just a place to see
fantastic scenery, although it certainly
has its share. Wyoming offers visitors a
chance to explore and to enrich them-
selves. It's a special place where having
fun and learning new things naturally
go hand in hand.

41

Beautifully Slow

There have been times when the population of Wyoming grew like wildfire. One time occurred after the turn of the century, from 1900 to 1930. Another was in the 1970s. At other times Wyoming grew at about the same rate as the rest of the country. But in the 1960s, its population didn't grow at all, and in the 1980s the population of the state actually shrank. Some people were very concerned. They wanted economic progress. They wanted industry. They wanted Wyoming to grow.

Even with its two periods of rapid development, Wyoming has remained a state of few people. It is the ninth-largest state in the country in area, but it has fewer than five people per square mile. Only Alaska, which is six times the size of Wyoming, has fewer people per square mile.

But when the people who wanted population growth looked at the rest of the country, they began to change their minds. People in industrial areas

odgepole pines are among the primary species of timber crops sed in Wyoming's lumber industry. Wyoming's forests cover .8 million acres, or about 16 percent of the state's total land area.

The rugged mountains of Yellowstone National Park provide a protected habitat for the majestic bighorn sheep.

elsewhere worried about the cost of growth. Factories filled the air with dirt and smoke. They put undesirable chemicals into the water and often created highly toxic waste products. Many people in other states wished they had not destroyed their forests and polluted their rivers in the name of progress.

In comparison, Wyoming began to look very good to the people who lived there. Things were slow in Wyoming—and they are today. It is still beautiful, still wild, still full of the wonders of nature. Nearly everywhere, the air is clear, and the water is clean.

As they move into the twenty-first century, the people of Wyoming are determined to protect the beauty of their state. Of course they want new businesses, jobs, and a certain amount of industry. Every state needs these things to remain economically healthy. But the people of Wyoming are not willing to sacrifice the benefits they have today.

What people all over the country look for, Wyoming still has. What people in factory towns and big cities have lost, Wyoming still has. And the unspoiled beauty that drew the early pioneers and settlers still exists in Wyoming.

807 John Colter, a member of the Lewis and Clark expedition, enters Wyoming and visits Yellowstone.

811 The Astorians cross the Bighorn Mountains and the Continental Divide.

812 Robert Stuart and his group build the first European-style building in the state.

824 The Rocky Mountain Fur Company, under William Ashley and Andrew Henry, announces discovery of the South Pass, which had already been known to Robert Stuart.

832 Captain Benjamin L. E. Bonneville builds Fort Bonneville on the Green River.

834 Robert Campbell and William Sublette build Fort William, the first permanent pioneer settlement in Wyoming, at the junction where the Platte and Laramie rivers cross.

835 Samuel Parker and Marcus Whitman attend the Grand Rendezvous on the Green River, at which Parker preached what was probably the first Protestant sermon in the Rockies.

842 Jim Bridger builds Fort Bridger on Black Forks of the Green River. John C. Frémont leads the first government expedition into the area.

843 Marcus Whitman brings the first large group of farming settlers over the Oregon Trail to Wyoming.

849 The United States government buys Fort Laramie.

851 The Great Treaty Council meets at Fort Laramie.

866 The Sioux lead Captain William J. Fetterman's troops into an ambush.

1868 The Shoshone are put on the Wind River Reservation. The Union Pacific Railroad crosses Wyoming. Congress creates the Wyoming Territory.

1872 Yellowstone Park is established.

1877 Chief Washakie of the Shoshone allows the Arapaho to stay at Wind River until a reservation is arranged for them.

1885 The first of three bad winters causes large cattle losses. Homesteaders move onto the open range.

1890 Wyoming becomes the 44th state.

1892 The Johnson County War breaks out after a dispute over cattle rustling.

1909 Five cattlemen go to prison for killing three sheepherders in the Ten Sleep Raid.

1924 Nellie Tayloe Ross is elected the first woman governor in the United States.

1929 Grand Teton National Park is established.

1949 Uranium deposits are discovered in Crook County.

1960 The nation's first intercontinental ballistic missile (ICBM) base is established near Cheyenne.

1976 A United States Supreme Court ruling allows extensive strip mining.

1988 A devastating forest fire damages large areas of Yellowstone National Park.

1995 In response to sheepherders' pleas, the Wyoming legislature introduces a series of bills to limit the number of gray wolves, which are federally protected.

The state seal on a buffalo symbolizes the branding of livestock. The red border represents both the Native Americans and the blood of the pioneers. On the state seal, the woman stands for equal rights, and the cowboy and the miner on either side represent the state's livestock and mining industries.

Wyoming Almanac

Nickname. The Equality State

Capital. Cheyenne

State Bird. Western meadowlark

State Flower. Indian paintbrush

State Tree. Cottonwood

State Motto. Equal Rights

State Song. "Wyoming"

State Abbreviations. Wyo. (traditional); WY (postal)

Statehood. July 10, 1890, the 44th state

Government. Congress: U.S. senators, 2; U.S. representatives, 1; State Legislature: senators, 30; representatives, 60; Counties: 23

Area. 97,914 sq mi (253,596 sq km), 9th in size among the states

Greatest Distances. north/south, 275 mi (443 km); east/west, 365 mi (587 km)

Elevation. Highest: Gannett Peak, 13,804 ft (4,208 m). Lowest: Belle Fourche River, 3,100 ft (945 m)

Population. 1990 Census: 455,975 (2.9% decrease since 1980), 50th among the states. Density: 5 persons per sq mi (2 persons per sq km). Distribution: 63% urban, 37% rural. 1980 Census: 469,557

Economy. *Agriculture:* cattle, sheep, hay, sugar beets, wheat, barley, corn, beans, oats, potatoes. *Manufacturing:* petroleum products, chemical products, food products, wood products, stone, clay and glass products. *Mining:* petroleum, coal, bentonite, natural gas, trona (sodium carbonate), clay, gemstones, sand, gypsum

State Seal

State Flower:
Indian paintbrush

State Bird:
Western meadowlark

Annual Events

★ Wyoming State Winter Fair in Lander (February)

★ Old West Days in Jackson (May)

★ Mountain Platte Bridge Encampment in Casper (June)

★ State Championship Chili Cook-Off in Chugwater (mid-June)

★ Central Wyoming Fair and Rodeo in Casper (July)

★ Frontier Days in Cheyenne (July)

★ Indian Sun Dances in Ethete and Fort Washakie (July)

★ Jubilee Days in Laramie (July)

★ Basque Festival in Buffalo (early August)

★ Indian pageant in Thermopolis (August)

★ State Fair in Douglas (August)

★ Fall Arts Festival in Jackson Hole (September)

★ Labor Day Pow Wow in Ethete (September)

Places to Visit

★ Bighorn National Forest in north-central Wyoming

★ Bridger-Teton National Forest in western Wyoming

★ Buffalo Bill Historical Center in Cody

★ Devils Tower National Monument in northeastern Wyoming

★ Fort Bridger State Historical Site, near Lyman

★ Fort Laramie National Historic Site, near Fort Laramie

★ Grand Teton National Park in northwestern Wyoming

★ Independence Rock State Historic Site, southwest of Casper

★ Medicine Lodge State Archaeological Site, near Hyattville

★ Wind River Canyon, near Thermopolis

★ Yellowstone National Park in northwestern Wyoming

Index